And the Good News Is...

Lessons and Advice from the Bright Side

: This is a quick read summary based on the novel "And the Good News Is..." by Dana Perino

D1050294

NOTE TO READERS:

This is a Summary & Analysis of And the Good News Is... Lessons and Advice from the Bright Side, by Dana Perino. You are encouraged to buy the full version.

TABLE OF CONTENTS

OVERVIEW

This in-depth book review of *And the Good News Is...Lessons and Advice from the Bright Side* by Dana Perino offers a detailed summary that mirrors the structure of the book followed by an analysis of the work. This book offers an historical sketch of the author's life including her childhood in Wyoming and a sketch of the twists and turns of her impressive career. In addition, the book is peppered with career advice and professional etiquette that Perino has gleaned from her extensive work with exceptional people.

The first chapter of the book is the longest and offers a detailed view of her family, her childhood, and her educational years through college. The second chapter follows the early years of her marriage and the career decisions leading up to her role as White House press secretary. Chapter three focuses on her work while press secretary, and chapter four is centered on her time as cohost on *The Five*. Chapter five explores various advice that Perino has found very helpful in her professional journey that she wants to pass on to her readers. Chapter six investigates the theme of civility in political discourse, and the final chapter offers insight into what Perino considers foundational to conservative thinking and her own attraction to those ideas.

Dana Perino is most known for her work as the first female Republican White House press secretary from September 2007 to January of 2009. She went on to be one of the several colorful hosts of Fox News' *The Five,* where she still works as a conservative political commentator.

SUMMARY

INTRODUCTION

In the opening section of the book, the author recounts a story from her last few months as press secretary for President George W. Bush. The incident took place in December 2008 during a presidential trip to Afghanistan and Iraq. For security reasons the trip was covert, and only a select handful of press had any knowledge of the plans. The president was having a press conference with the Prime Minister of Iraq, Nouri al-Maliki for both the American journalists that had been privy to the trip as wells as several Iraqi journalists. A few minutes into opening remarks one of the Iraqi journalists took off his shoes and hurled them at President Bush. In his rush to protect the President, a member of security rushed the podium and banged the mic boom which swung and hit Perino in the face.

After Iraqi security had the man in custody, President Bush resumed the press conference. Meanwhile Perino got some ice for her face from the staff doctor, Dr. Richard Tubb. However, with a tight schedule to keep she went back to work preparing President Bush for an interview with ABC reporter Martha Raddatz before retiring to Air Force One for some rest. After awaking from a nap, the blood had pooled at the site of the injury giving Perino a nasty swollen black eye. The next stop was Kabul where first the team was met with hundreds of U.S. troops, followed by a visit with President of Afghanistan, Hamid Karzai. Perino joined President Bush to greet President

Karzai, who knew about the shoe incident and shared in some banter about the black eye. The black eye was with Perino for the last six weeks of the Bush administration and Perino's tenure as White House press secretary.

Perino then turns to the book more generally and shares the goals and purposes of the book. She was the first and only press secretary that was a woman and a Republican and she served during a busy time in terms of both domestic issues and foreign relations. She tried to speak for the President and the country in ways that would represent honor, grace and dignity and make the President proud of her words and tone. The book is about what she was thinking and feeling during this time, which includes her optimistic outlook, hence the book name. Her optimistic nature melded well with the President's outlook and gave them good chemistry as a team. The book covers the road to the White House, her tenure as press secretary, and her work as a news pundit afterwards. She also hopes to share the wisdom and advice she has gained by great people she has come into contact with in her family and professional life. She shares tips that have helped her with her professional and personal success. She hopes that the book will inspire readers to see that no matter what their individual background is, they can achieve great things.

CHAPTER 1: WIDE-OPEN SPACES

Perino opens this chapter with a vignette from the President's last visit with the Navy SEALs before Obama's inauguration. She describes the President as very much enamored with the SEALs. He demonstrated a deep bond with the men in these elite forces. After delivering a speech, the President shook each of their hands and posed for a picture with them. The overall effect of the description is one of a bittersweet moment at the end of their time working together.

The author then turns to her childhood. She was born in Evanston, a small community in the southwest corner of Wyoming. Her parents, Leo Ernest Perino and Janice Marie Brooks, were cattle ranchers. Although they moved to Colorado when Perino was two, they were frequent visitors to Wyoming and so she talks of her native state of Colorado-Wyoming. Perino links her sense of individualism, patriotism and love of freedom to her upbringing in the West. Her great-grandparents left Italy for America. On her father's side they were poor farm workers and coal miners. They received 320 acres of land under the Enlarged Homestead Act. Her great-grandfather died of black lung during the 1960's. Her great-grandmother, Rosi, had seven children while managing the ranch. She lived to be 100, and the night she died, Perino had a dream of her death. She came to believe this was her great-grandmother's way of saying goodbye.

Her grandpa, Leo Perino Sr. was born in 1921 and was the second youngest of Rosi's children. He grew up on the ranch, and was a Marine who fought in the Pacific during WWII. He met her grandmother Vicky while serving in Philadelphia and after his service she followed him to the Black Hills. Perino Sr.

and his siblings increased the acreage of the ranch over the years as more land to buy became available. It reached 50,000 acres at the peak of its size.

Her father, who now lives in Denver, was the oldest of three boys that grew up ranching. She spent her first few years on the ranch along with uncles Matt and Tom and their families. She describes an idyllic childhood on the ranch with her cousins. They had chores but also plenty of outdoor fun. The ranch was also full of animals of all kinds: horses, chickens, dogs, pigs, cats, cattle, and peacocks. Particular favorites among her memories were some of the stand out dogs which she describes in some detail. After moving to Denver, her family still visited the ranch several times a year. Although she and her sister helped their cousins with specific chores, they did not have a lot of responsibility on visits to the ranch. Other adventures included fossil hunting, winter sledding, playing on the trampoline, and joining her grandpa on emergencies putting brush fires out on the prairies. An interesting historical tidbit is that the ranch was chosen as a site for the Marlboro ads from the 19070's.

Perino also had a pony at the ranch named Sally. And there were other horses as well, including a fancy racehorse used to breed speed into the horse stock on the ranch. There were hard life lessons on the ranch as well. One day while out doing rounds they came across one of the horses with a broken leg. Just small girls, Perino and her sister were told to duck down and not look while their grandfather shot the suffering animal. Although traumatic at the time, she argues this taught her the lesson that being strong and being gentle go together. The fondest memory Perino details from her childhood at the ranch was the yearly cattle drive.

After college Perino visited the ranch less often due to her schedule and the distance. Her husband, Peter McMahon, joined one year for the spring cattle drive. Her grandfather was a county commissioner and was one of her early political mentors. There was often news playing on the television or radio and her grandfather engaged her in discussions about current events and shared his conservative political views. Her grandparents also has a strong and loving relationship. He died in 2001 of a massive heart attack while working the cattle. Her grandmother died in 2010. They were both strong patriots and very proud of their American life.

Her maternal grandparents were from Kansas and Texas. Grandmother Dorothy and Grandfather Thomas married before he fought in WWII. He worked for a laundry company and later a bank before opening an insurance business, a gas station, a motel and an apartment building. In later years they lived In Rawlins, Wyoming. The author shares some fond memories of her grandmother who was well known for her baking, sewing and good fashion sense. Perino appreciated and learned from the traditional division of labor in the relationship that her grandparents had and shares that some of the success of her own marriage has its roots in clearly established responsibilities. Another lesson she learned from her grandparents, who grew up in the depression, is just how good America is in comparison to other countries. Patriotism was a strong theme for her maternal grandparents.

Perino's mother, Janice Marie Brooks, grew up helping at the motel with her younger sister Patty Sue, but also participating in school activities such as sports and band. She recalls a story from when her mother and her band mates got up and left at a restaurant along a road trip to a game that would not serve the single black student among the athletes. Janice did not tolerate racism. She was also quite the piano player. She attended college and worked in health care. She also did volunteer work with an organization that helped refugees get settled in the United States. Many of them were from communist countries and from spending some time with them Perino was exposed to the oppressive circumstances many of the refugees had fled.

Her father, Leo Perino Jr. was born into ranching but dissatisfied with it, in part due to allergies and also a love for business. He went to college at Casper College, where he met Janice, and worked in human resources. After they married, the couple lived about 20 miles from the ranch in a town called Newcastle, Wyoming. They stayed in one of the rentals her maternal grandparents owned. He was called by the draft but did not serve due to an ulcer. They moved to Evantson, Wyoming and her dad taught classes in business to State Hospital patients. He took graduate classes at Utah State University. Her father was successful and they moved to Denver, Colorado where he worked for Western Farm Bureau Life Insurance Company. Perino and her father read and discussed news stories as early as the third grade. The also shared news programs and magazines. Politics was a part of Perino's life even as a child.

When she was four her sister Angela Leigh was born. When she got a little bit older her two big interests were the fashion of the 80's and reading. She had piano lessons, gymnastic practice, and choir. When she was seven years old a trip to Washington D.C. with her parents, including a trip to the White House, made an impression on her. Although many of her school experiences were positive, she had a difficult year in the fourth grade. In an effort to integrate schools, Denver bussed kids into different neighborhoods and Perino was one of five white children in her grade. She was tormented and bullied by the other kids and it was a very difficult experience for her. Her parents moved to the suburbs of Parker, Colorado which solved her issues at school.

High school was better and she was popular with many friends. She made excellent grades and did not get in much trouble. She was class president, and was very active with the speech team. She went to a smaller school for college at the urging of her father. She chose University of Sothern Colorado because of the smaller classes, the opportunity to work at the public television station there, and a full tuition scholarship on the speech team. She graduated with honors. She went to graduate school at the University of Illinois Springfield in the public affairs reporting program. She interned with a local CBS affiliate but found it difficult because of what she perceived to be a liberal media bias. After graduate school she returned home with her parents, waiting tables and looking for the right opportunity. While applying for another position, she called the staff of Representative Scott McInnis, whom she had interviewed a few times while working at PBS in college. Instead of a reference, he offered her a job working in Washington D. C.

She moved into a townhouse with some Democrat roommates that were mean to her. The living situation did not last long. Her political positions were gradually forming, but she was strongly drawn to ideas of small government, the idea of personal responsibility and a well-funded defense budget. The book *What I Saw at the Revolution* by Peggy Noonan in which Noonan describes her work as Ronald Reagan's speech writer, was a major turning point for Perino. The book helped her to recognize core principles of conservative logic and that it was okay to be both a woman and a Republican. Noonan became an important intellectual guide for Perino, and later in her career she interviewed Noonan while working on Fox, and the two became friends.

Perinio's work in Washington started with greeting people to the Capitol. Despite not being a glorious job, it is where she started building contacts that would eventually enable her work as press secretary for the White House. Within a few months she met Tim Rutten at a hockey game and during the course of conversation found out about an opportunity open for a press secretary for Rep. Dan Schaefer from Colorado, which she landed. There she found a mentor in the chief of staff, Holly Propst who taught her about writing press releases and handling journalists. In 1997, while working on an assignment for Congressman Schaefer, Perino met her husband.

CHAPTER 2: LOVE AT FIRST FLIGHT

Perino was 25 years old in 1997. Despite having achieved a degree of professional success and making progress on financial stability, she was still struggling with confidence and spent a great deal of time worrying. Her ambitious drive was telling her it was time to make another move up, but she was not sure where that would be. She did not follow the path of working as a lobbyist, which many with the strong contacts she had cultivated are apt to do, however, she was not sure what to do next. Meanwhile, the romantic front had stalled due to what Perino describes as slim pickings among Washington's single men. She describes this period as a quarter life crisis that many women feel at this point in their life where childhood dreams aren't quite coming true. She was active socially with her church and did volunteer work as well, but she was worried about being in a rut.

In August she took a flight from Denver back to D.C. and on that flight was her future husband, Peter McMahon. The two were seated next to each other on the flight and what started as a topical conversation about the book he was reading turned to more personal topics such as their upbringings and how they shared a political world view. Peter had several qualities that struck Perino such as a kind of rugged masculinity that showed through his British accent and mannerisms, the fact that he was well traveled, and his love for dogs. Most of all, he made her laugh. She describes that by the flight's end she was already feeling the gravity of love for this older, English man. They exchanged contact information.

Peter wrote her an email expressing that he had been thinking of her often, as well as some candid emotional expressions, but it got lost due to a service provider change. Meanwhile, Perino had mailed him a postcard that was sitting at his office for a few days before he found out about it. Both spent the time thinking the other had already forgotten about the encounter. Once Peter realized the email had bounced he sent it again, and just about the time that Perino had decided to move on, she got it. For a while they conducted a long distance romance with email and phone. Peter was, after all, living in England. Then they made a plan to meet in New Orleans. After a romantic weekend, Peter anxiously disclosed that he had a vasectomy so that if her future plans included having children it would be a deal breaker. But Perino had already decided that she did not want to have children so the air was cleared. The two both had a sense that they would be together from then on. Within two months, they had decided she would move to England, and within nine months of their original meet, she did.

She moved in with Peter in a town called Lytham St. Annes and had no professional responsibilities. She read, did some cooking, took some fitness classes, toured the countryside, got a puppy, and volunteered. A year from their meeting they were engaged and soon eloped. However, she soon got restless. There were not many opportunities for her to use her professional skill set in England and by 1999 they decided to move back to the States, and chose San Diego, in part because of the contrast in the weather from dreary old England. The move was very spontaneous. Peter was able to borrow some money to start a business and Perino exercised some contacts she had made in Washington to get a job at the City Hall and later several public relations companies. When money stress was making her worry all the time, she turned those concerns over to Peter, and she describes this as giving her an empowering freedom.

In 2000 an opportunity came up to be a spokesperson for the Bush campaign in California, which she did not take because the pay and benefits were not enough. After a long discussion with Peter, the couple decided that she simply would not be satisfied until she was back working in D.C. She planned a trip to D.C. to get in touch with her contacts there and let them know she was looking for an opportunity in Washington. A week before the trip was planned 9/11 happened. She and Peter watched in horror from their living room. Perino was calmed by Bush's response to the crisis, and it made her even more determined to serve in his administration in some capacity. Within a few days of 9/11, one of her contacts at the Justice Department offered her an opportunity to work with their public affairs team, which she gladly took.

She adjusted to the work quickly. A good deal of the job involved discussing, or rather avoiding discussing, the details of active DOJ cases with reporters. Several of the cases she worked were environmental cases. It was not the most glorious work, particularly for a Republican during a time of terrorism, however, she knew that shining at this work was an opportunity to be noticed. It paid off. Jim Connaughton, who was running the Council on Environmental Quality (CEQ) at the White House, invited her onto the team, drawing her closer to the White House communications team. Here she got to know the current press secretary, Ari Fleischer, and the future press secretary Scott McClellan. President Bush won the 2004 elections, which secured her position at the CEQ, but she was again getting restless. Soon after, McClellan offered her the deputy press secretary job for the White House team, which she gleefully accepted.

CHAPTER 3: STEPPING UP TO THE PODIUM

Perino was deputy press secretary for about two and a half years of extreme pressure and endless work when the White House chief of staff, Josh Bolten, addressed the staff suggesting that anyone that was feeling burnt out might consider leaving since the President wanted a strong last few years and needed an energized team. Perino was torn. Here marriage was certainly strained from the workload, but she also had a tremendous loyalty to the Bush administration and felt truly challenged by the work. She decided to leave the job. She went back to work after a short vacation and arranged a meeting to tell Ed Gillespie the news. Before she got her resignation on the table, Gillespie offered her the White House press secretary job. She was stunned.

The news was somewhat bittersweet because of the circumstances surrounding the then press secretary, Tony Snow, who was leaving the office due to pressing health concerns and a long fight with colon cancer. Perino had some doubts about why she was selected, specifically worrying that the offer was more about convenience than her specific qualifications and confidence in her abilities. She was assured it was the latter, and accepted the position. At the press briefing on the turnover, President Bush went off notes to express a sincere sentiment that his selection was based on his confidence in Perino's abilities.

Perino shares a funny story about her first weeks as press secretary. The podium in the briefing room was built for Snow, who is 6'5" and Perino is an even 5'. Determined not to be a bother, she had insisted on just standing on a box behind the podium, and only later found out that the angle of the camera, unless drawn for a wide angle, made her head cover part of the seal on the wall behind her, revealing "The White Ho." She agreed to have a new podium constructed more appropriate to her height.

In 2008, Perino joined President Bush on a tour of the Middle East, and the president's first trip to Israel. The hopes for the trip included peace talks between Israeli Prime Minister Olmert and Palestinian Presidet Abbas. At a formal dinner with the Israeli cabinet she had an opportunity to witness Bush's decisive leadership. After a speech by the Prime Minister he declared to the cabinet that if anyone at the table was not prepared to support the peace accord that the Prime Minister was backing, then they should speak up now, because the U.S. was not going to be embarrassed by a breakdown in negotiations due to internal disputes in the Israeli cabinet. He then engaged them in conversation about their backgrounds and managed to encourage the delegates to see their common mission in serving the interests of Israel and simultaneously building camaraderie around the goals of the peace talks. Perino was floored with respect for the President.

She also shares of a heart wrenching visit with critically wounded veterans with President Bush in 2005 where he showed an incredible connection with the troops offering true compassion. Most of the families were grateful for his visit, but one mother was angry and the President stood and allowed her to vent her anger. On the plane later he shared with Perino that he thought she had a right to be angry. Her account shows a deeply human side of President Bush as a man who took his role as Commander in Chief to heart.

In 2008, former White House press secretary Scott McClellan wrote a book that was received as fairly negative concerning

President Bush. McClellan had left the press secretary position after a host of difficult situations for the Bush administration including criticism of the response to Hurricane Katrina and investigations of Scooter Libby and Karl Rove. Although President Bush understood the difficulties faced by McClellan due to the issues of the times, the press had become antagonistic with him and there were issues of trust and rapport that were breaking down. A decision was made that a change in the position was critical to establishing a better relationship with the press. The book was indeed critical of the administration. Because of her own loyalties to the President, Perino was very disturbed about the book. The President called her in the office and personally persuaded her to forgive McClellan. She was deeply moved.

Another personal story that Perino recounts of her time with the President includes his interest in the families of his staffers and his thoughtful attention to detail on such matters. After her parents divorced in 2000, Perino's relationship with her father was somewhat strained. Aware of this fact, President Bush took special note that Perino had invited her father to one of the White House dinners. He went out of his way to greet her father and introduce him to several people at the dinner. He also bragged about the great work that Perino was doing. Perino credits this intervention by President Bush with saving her relationship with her father. Overall her memories of serving as White House press secretary are fond, and her loyalty to President George W. Bush unwavering.

CHAPTER 4: THE FIVE

The CEO of Fox News, Roger Ailes, originally imagined *The Five* to be a temporary filler for the 5p.m. slot which opened when Glen Beck left. The vision for the show was to have people with different backgrounds have the kind of discussion about politics that had the feel of family. Despite being a tough time slot, the show was successful from the start and the decision was made to make it a permanent fixture. Perino was ready for a change after the work as press secretary and the show at Fox was a great fit. Prior to the call for the show, Perino had many irons in many fires and was feeling stretched thin on a variety of projects that had little overall coherence. Choosing her for the show was based on previous work she did as a weekly guest on Hannity's show on the same network.

The transition from speaking for the President, and having her own voice distinct from the administration did take some work, but Perino overcame. In stark contrast to her work as press secretary, the formula for success at *The Five* included letting herself be known and familiar as a person to the audience. Over the years she has come to let her guard down and express humor and other emotional sides to herself that had no place in her previous work.

Another adjustment for Perino was the level of contention on the show. Her preference is for consensus building and trying to resolve conflict, but she has had to learn that it is okay to participate in heated debate, and that she and her cohosts don't have to agree. She then gives a brief overview of each of her cohosts in turn. Kimberly Guilfoyle is a single mother and former educator, prosecutor and model. Here legal expertise is particularly helpful on the show, and her antagonistic chemistry with Bob is often entertaining. Andrea Tantaros is no longer a host on the show but a regular visitor. The daughter of successful Greek immigrants who now own several businesses, she believes in self-reliance and hard work to achieve the American Dream. She also has a background as a publicist and was a columnist for the *New York Daily News*. Juan Williams is a journalist that worked at *The Washington Post* and NPR, among others and specializes in covering race relations. Eric Bolling started his career as a baseball player but soon had to give it up due to an injury at which time he took a chance on a job in finance, and worked hard to build financial security for his family. He also knew many victims of the 9/11 attacks personally and has a passion for national security issues as a result. Greg Gutfeld and Perino share a deep sense of humor. She also describes him as fearless and a reminder for her to let loose a little. Bob Beckel is quite the character, and many viewers either love him or hate him. A recovering addict and the only left minded host on the show, Beckel often the target of some extra teasing. Perino describes him as very good natured.

Overall, Perino describes being on *The Five*, as more fulfilling than she expected it to be. She has been pleased with the sense of impact that she feels the show has on national political perspectives because of its large audience. She also appreciates the viewer mail and comments about the show. She attributes the success of the show with the chemistry of the hosts.

Near the close of the chapter, Perino takes a moment to share about her two dogs. First is Henry, the Hungarian Vizsla, who she got as a puppy while living in England. The move to New York was a difficult transition for the old dog and not long after she moved he died. During his time, however, he was a great companion, and she taught him many funny tricks. The night he died, a call from Greta Van Susteren convinced her and husband Peter that getting a new puppy immediately was the best thing to do. They called a breeder of Vizslas, and named their puppy Jasper even before she and Peter picked him up. Jasper visited *The Five* on his second day home. Eternal nemesis of Bob, many fans enjoy Jasper's visits to the show.

CHAPTER 5: TAKE IT FROM ME – PLEASE

One of the service projects that Perino has taken on over the years is developing a program she likens to the speed dating equivalent of mentoring, called Minute Mentoring. The unique process of the program was that women leaders were paired with small groups of mentees, they then shared three pieces of advice that have been helpful to them in their lives, answered some questions, and then the mentees switched mentors. Originally conceived of as a way target professionally minded women, the program later opened to both genders. Her vision for the book also included a place to pass on some of the advice from the program and from her own life and so this chapter is devoted to that topic. Here is the advice she offers with brief explanations:

- "Making butterflies fly in formation." This advice was given to Perino by her speech coach in college, Shawnalee Whitney. It referred to the idea that nerves can be a good thing before public speaking as long as they are funneled in healthy ways and contribute to the energy of the performance.
- "Find your strong voice." By this Perino is referring to not talking as if everything is a question, also known as up-talking, and rather be assertive with your speech. She traces the roots of this to teen culture and the benefit it has to be confrontational avoidant in those spaces. But the down side is that it works against confidence and the perception that you have something important to say. Children, she argues, need

to be broken of this habit or it can have dire career consequences.

- "Ban the explanation point." Perino argues that excessive use of emotional expression, such as explanation points, emoji's or emoticons in professional email discredits the author and she recommends against it. On a related note she suggests keeping each email to one subject for easier tracking.
- "No Ugg boots at the office." The point here is that people should dress for the next rung up the ladder in their careers.
- "Spit it out (Your gum, that is)." Gum chewing is just unprofessional.
- "Always take your husband's phone calls." Family matters and this is one way to make your significant other know their place in your life. Managers can encourage this behavior by being sensitive to employees needs in this area.
- "Speak up when it counts." It is important to know which issues are worth raising. Speaking up over every little thing and people will tune you out. If it is something that could threaten business, for instance an ongoing safety issue, then it is important to speak up.
- "Share the credit." This was a lesson that Perino took from President Bush. Loyalty is built when you share credit with others.
- "Loyalty – A two-way-street." When loyalty goes both ways, trust can be built.
- "Be willing to take the blame for your team." She recounts a harsh campaign loss during the 2000 election. Then Governor Bush took full responsibility for the loss with the campaign staff. It built strong loyalty among the staffers.

- "Stick up for others – even when they don't know it." The main argument here is that it is just the morally right thing to do.
- "Why, thank you very much." Handwritten thank-you notes communicate sincerity. Email is not enough. Particularly for young job interviewers, a hand written note can help them stand out from the competition.
- "Reverse mentors." Young people well versed in rapid technological change can be very helpful with bosses that are often older and may be less well fluent with the latest technology. Offering help without judgment is a way to build loyalty.
- "Zip it." Listening is sometimes the best move a person can make. Knowing when to listen is important, even though it seems a rare quality these days.
- "Let it go." Wasting time and energy on little things saps energy that can be better spent in other more productive ways.
- "Pass it on." At work your coworkers can one day be your boss or your employee so treating them well pays off in the long run because you can build allies. Mentoring younger staff is another way to give back to the environment of your workplace.
- "To school or not to school?" To this question Perino suggest that the answer is complicated and very context dependent on a person's goals. She suggests taking a strong and detailed inventory of life goals to consider the cost of school and weighing it against the benefits. It should not be a decision based on having nothing better to do.
- "Move out to move up." Consistent with her own career trajectory, Perino advises that moving to new opportunities that offer an advancement is important for career success and to overcome the fear of making

such moves. Parents also need to be aware about pressuring their kids to stay near their home towns where opportunities may be limited.

- "It's okay to leave a big dog employer, too." Sometimes progress can be slow at top notch companies where jobs are in high demand and people seldom leave them. Being willing to go somewhere else to find new experiences that will broaden a person's overall portfolio and lead to advancement is an important strategy.

- "Get out of town." Here Perino stresses the importance of travel to broaden horizons and make yourself a more interesting person.

- "Feed your brain." Reading news and literature gives you a broader view and allows you to be informed of the world while increasing your ability to connect with other people.

- "You are who you meet." Look for networking events, attend them, and have questions ready that will start conversations based on people's interests. Keeping in touch with friends made over the years with the occasional hand written note keeps contacts active.

- "Take responsibility for the one thing you can control – your health." Healthy choices have to be a priority even when other demands are pressing. When health is pushed off, everything else will eventually suffer too.

- "Balance is in the eye of the beholder." Balance is hard to achieve, but important. Keeping good and detailed schedules, learning when to say no, and accepting our limitations are all key to finding balance.

- "What's the worst that could happen?" We need to take risks to be successful in life. Sometimes assessing risk is really about looking at what the fears are behind it and realizing they may be all acceptable losses.

- "What do you do for fun?" Having things that are just for fun are important for your mental and spiritual health, as well as giving you interesting things to share with other people.
- "Love is not a career-limiting decision." Our family is important and it is okay when love is a priority in our lives.

CHAPTER 6: CIVILITY, LOST AND FOUND

Perino starts this chapter by remembering a visit with all five living presidents at a special dinner prior to President Obama's inauguration. President Bush wanted to be sure that the White House welcomed the new president. Despite deep political differences, the five men found the ability to have dignity and respect for one another. Her concern here is that America is losing a tone of civility of days past and that current partisan bickering is damaging, and is even more concerned about in party fighting, particularly among Republicans.

The author argues that being civil does not mean that parties cannot disagree, rather, everyone loses when personal insults start getting thrown about. One thing she suggests is to try to keep in mind that although we may be approaching the solutions from different perspectives, we are often trying to solve the same problems and have the same goals. Part of the context for why such uncivil tactics seem to be more the norm these days is a very crowded media environment where even our government officials are playing into sensationalism for attention.

Perino goes into some detail concerning the much maligned Bush administration's attempts to meet the vicious name calling with silence and to not respond in kind. This was difficult for Perino who had so much loyalty for the President. Still, she came to see that it was the right approach not to get embroiled in the mudslinging. It did not reward such behavior with more attention and headlines.

For Perino, being civil is an act of personal responsibility and one that she takes seriously. She tries to be sensitive to the ways that her words will be understood. It has been a process of trial and error, but a value she takes seriously. Manners too are closely related to being civil. There are times and places for political and religious conversations, and knowing when it is not appropriate, for example on purely social occasions, is important.

Responding to criticism is also important to Perino. In particular, due to the prevalence of social media, criticism is an almost constant feature of our lives now. She has some advice for the reader on how to handle this situation. The first thing is to turn off any search alerts for your name. If you are in a situation where your reputation is critical, then assign someone who works for you, or a friend, to keep an eye on the alerts to let you know if something really needs to be addressed. Generally the best plan of action is to simply ignore the criticism, according to Perino. Another strategy is to anticipate criticism, and include any rebuttal to that critique in your original statement or action. Restraining from overly defensive responses is also an important tool. Being the "bigger" person does translate to people that are paying attention. Humor, when witty, is another potential tool for responding to criticism.

How you compliment someone is also important. Underhanded compliments, are according to Perino, when someone combines an insult and a compliment, and then expects you to be grateful about it. She argues that if you can't just say something nice, then don't bother saying it at all. In addition, the tone a person takes when answering a contentious question matters. Just because someone disagrees with you does not mean you have to make a choice to have a hostile tone. Sarcasm too is not necessary, and is particularly destructive in professional settings. Self-deprecating jokes are a safer way to have humor without offending people or insulting them. Then Perino makes a point of sharing how a few Democrats such as President Obama and Vice President Joe Biden have embodied these qualities with her in several interactions over the years. She also mentions her close relationship with Donna Brazile, previous campaign manager for Al Gore. Although they have political disagreements, they have high regard for each other and treat each other with civility and respect.

CHAPTER 7: UNAFRAID TO BE RIGHT

In this brief chapter Perino summarizes the foundations of her conservative positions. She explains that her views did meander a bit in college, but that reading the work of Peggy Noonan solidified her conservative stance. Perino sees conservative thought to be based in logic, facts and reality, and liberal thought as based in emotions, theory and fantasies. She believes in a fixed moral code verses situational ethics. She believes in personal responsibility over the responsibility of the State. She also characterizes liberals as doctrinaire and rigid in their belief systems. She feels that conservatives are mistreated in general by the media, and unfairly so.

ONE MORE THING

This last section of the book is mainly a thank you to her many mentors along her journey and a final reminiscent moment of the last hours in office with President Bush.

ANALYSIS

And the Good News Is...Lessons and Advice from the Bright Side offers an overall optimistic perspective from former White House press secretary and current cohost of Fox News' The Five, Dana Perino. Unapologetically conservative in her views, those that identify as Republican are most likely to favorably receive this book. However, while others may not appreciate her negative view of liberals, they may still be interested in the colorful stories of behind-the-scenes moments from her time with the administration of President George W. Bush.

The first half of the book is focused on her background and the various career decisions she made while navigating her impressive career. The detail is rich and the storytelling is compelling. The reader will get a glimpse into the beauty of Western ranch living and the specific ideals of patriotism and visions of America that are cultivated there. The strong foundation for what would later become the basis for her ideological perspective clearly traces to her childhood and young adult life. The personal nature of many of the decisions she made throughout her career offer the reader a glimpse into who the author is on a very personal level. The reader will also get a sense for the character of this exceptional woman from this candid self-portrait.

Chapter five is particularly helpful for readers of any political persuasion as it offers sage advice from a highly successful veteran of the professional worlds of public relations, politics, and commentating. Perhaps of special inspiration to ambitious young women, the advice is fairly gender neutral and could be just as helpful to men. A special focus of her advice section is guidance towards building a network of allies as one moves through the ranks, something that Perino has clearly mastered over the course of her professional life. The advice is overall both practical and savvy, although at times it reads like a lecture in manners from a different time.

Critical readers are likely to notice two main flaws. The first is that Perino persistently notices and points to liberal bias, but frames conservative thinking as if it is neutral and objective. She is dismissive of the validity of liberal positions, characterizes them as irrational and fantasy based, and yet at no point in the work does she engage the substance of a single progressive idea. Related to this is the persistent positioning of conservatives as victims of hostility and what amounts to conspiracy level liberal media bias. Although this is a common narrative in conservative punditry, there is little evidence raised in the book to support this claim. The persuasiveness of Perino on this point basically relies on the regularity with which she repeats the assertion rather than any particularly sound arguments or evidence.

A second flaw in the book centers around Perino's extreme distaste for incivility in modern political discourse, detailed most explicitly in chapter six. While Perino is right to point out that such discourse is rife among both Democrats and Republicans, she is not fully able to acknowledge her own participation in nasty, petty and partisan grandstanding relative to her participation at Fox News, or more specifically on *The Five*, which is a show that receives high viewer ratings as a direct result of its conflict ridden and sound bite driven format. Although she has a few sentences acknowledging that some may critique her on this point, she offers no real response to the critique other than trying to personally distance herself from the effects of that show by suggesting her individual contributions have been less bombastic than others. The overall effect of the combination of her chapter long discussion of civility in politics, and her inability to see herself as part of the problem, is dissonant at best. Still, many readers will enjoy the stories and advice offered in this book. The writing is well done and the pace of the book keeps the reader's attention.

59014775R00022

Made in the USA
Middletown, DE
20 December 2017